Brainspotting with young people

# AN ADVENTURE
# INTO THE MIND

By Mark Grixti

Illustrated by Rosanna Dean

Foreword by David Grand, PhD

**Brainspotting with Young People**
**An Adventure into the Mind**

Text © Mark Grixti 2015
mark@grixti.co.uk

Illustrations © Rosanna Dean 2015

Published in Great Britain by Sattva

ISBNs
Hardback: 978-0-9934269-0-2
Paperback: 978-0-9934269-3-3
Kindle: 978-0-9934269-1-9
Epub: 978-0-9934269-2-6

## Acknowledgements

My thanks to Roman, TJ, MN and to all of the incredible young people who have inspired me and taught me so much.

# Foreword

"Where we look affects how we feel." Our traumas can be detected in our ordinary facial and eye reflexes, and by using these windows to inner mental states, emotional distress can be effectively relieved in adults and children.

Since discovering Brainspotting in my psychotherapy practice in 2003, I have spent many years developing and refining the approach. There are now many thousand clinicians across the United States, Europe, South America, Middle East and Asia using Brainspotting to ease human suffering and facilitate emotional healing.

Brainspotting is a brain-body therapy that relies heavily on the profound attunement with the therapist. Dr Mark Grixti is a psychologist with a background in systems thinking and it has come as no surprise to me that he has written this book that reflects his commitment to attunement with the client, which is evident through the playful rhyming narrative and the enchanting illustrations of the panda bears. This artistic combination provides the reader the first-hand experience of the power of 'right-brain function' that operates alongside conscious awareness resulting in a significant emotional experience. Or in other words, much like art, we know that love, empathy and attachment is experienced at an emotional level that is often beyond words.

Through a gentle, heartfelt and elegantly playful approach the reader gains an insight into the experience of trauma and the stages of good attachment-based therapy. With the support of Big Bear, Bear Cub agrees to accept some help. They call upon a black and white furry therapist, who with the aid of a bamboo stick, some music, and a cheeky parrot, helps Cub learn to make sense of difficult emotions, how to build up psychological resources and the amazing potential for the mind's repair through deeply attuned Brainspotting therapy.

*Brainspotting with Young People: An Adventure into the Mind* seeks to introduce a powerful and effective therapeutic tool in a playful, respectful and reassuring way. It is intended to encourage and enlighten children, families and therapists on their journey towards finding profound emotional healing.

David Grand, PhD
*Brainspotting: The Revolutionary New Therapy
for Rapid and Effective Change*
New York

# A BOOK ABOUT BRAINSPOTTING

This is a book about a bear
Quite young
Feeling upset and having no fun.

In this adventure
Bear Cub makes a discovery
Leading to healing and deep recovery.

Cub's discovery had a quizzical name
Do you think you can guess it
In a guessing game?

Not schnoozle or bamboozle
Or dollop or splodge
Not gargoyle or giggles
Hogwash or hodgepodge!

The answer to this quiz?
Bear Cub found...
BRAINSPOTTING
Now how does that sound?

It may sound strange
Unusual I suppose
So let's wait no further and see how it goes...

# BEAR CUB FEELS UPSET

Bear Cub had been feeling unhappy and sad
Feeling real weird
And thinking real bad.

"Oh Cubby" purred Big Bear
"You have had some hard times
But you are safe now
And Cub – so am I."

"I have an idea that I think you will like
We can go see a *therapist*
That will help you feel right."

*"A 'Hairy-Beast' sounds scary*
*This doesn't sound right!"*

Gasped the young Bear Cub
Clinging on tight.

"Not **hairy-beast** but therapist"
Bear said nice and slow
"A kind helpful person
Who helps these things go."

Bear Cub was still worried
And did not look glad
"They might think I'm silly or stupid or mad!"

Big Bear then said gently
"Why you are no fool
When you're struggling with something
Getting help is real cool!"

# MEETING THE THERAPIST

...and his parrot !!

The next day the pandas
Crossed town heading east
For the first appointment
With the kind 'hairy-beast'.

Who wasn't that hairy at all as it goes
Just black and white fur
From black ears to black toes.

"I am happy to meet you
Sit down anywhere"
Said the kind therapist
As the bears chose their chairs.

"You can call me Doc"
That was an easier word
And then Cub spotted the most colourful bird.

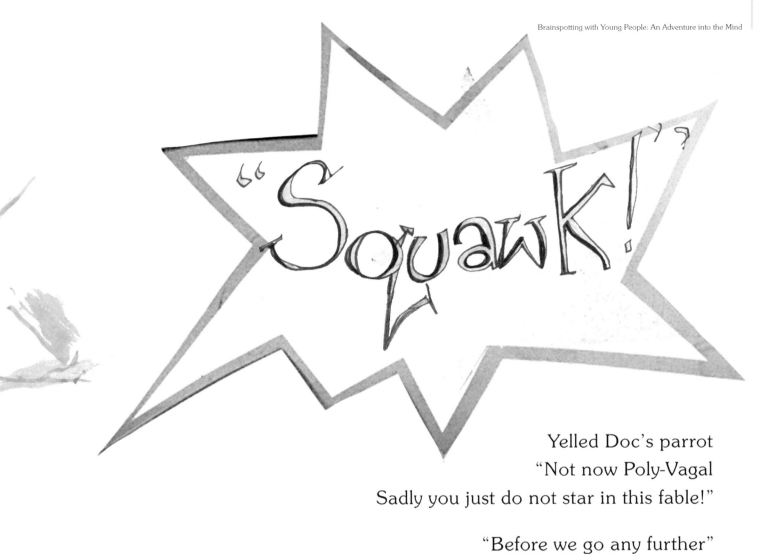

Yelled Doc's parrot
"Not now Poly-Vagal
Sadly you just do not star in this fable!"

"Before we go any further"
Doc carried on
"Perhaps you can tell me
What makes you feel strong?"

Cub was surprised and smiled big and gappy
Talking about hobbies
Always made Cub feel happy.

*"I can run*

*climb*

*and jump"*

Cub began to explain
"When I'm having fun
I am strong with no pain!"

"This is good" Doc said
"When you feel like yourself
This is the key to improving your health."

# CUB LEARNS SOMETHING VERY SPECIAL

"In your head is a brain," said Doc
It's amazingly clever
It remembers everything for ever and ever."

"And your *eyes* are wise
They help the brain handle more"
Doc then asked the question
"What colour's your front door?"

Without meaning to
Cub's eyes knew what to do
They found a position quite new
**"Why that's easy it's blue!"**

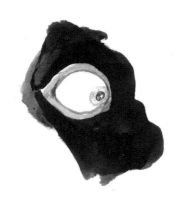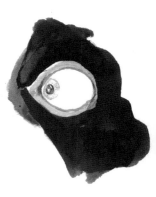

"Grrrreat!" said the Doc
"Your *eyes* knew where to go
To find the right answer
Right, left, high or low!"

Cub's furry face
Was now starting to smile
Both eyes on one spot
As Cub thought for a while.

Doc told the Bear Cub
"There's another thing I do
I hold up a stick of the finest bamboo."

"Can I eat it?"
Asked Bear Cub
With a wink of an eye...

Dreaming of ice-cream and hot bamboo pie.

"Perhaps later" said Doc
Holding up the bamboo
"This stick helps your eyes
Find the memories too."

"One more thing" Doc told Cub
"We can get help from your ears
You can listen to music
And this eases the fears."

First eyes and now ears
Cub had learned much that day
With the headphones in place
Looking like a DJ!

This sounded okay
Especially the songs
Then Bear Cub cried
"I might get it all wrong?"

"What if I can't look?" Cub said
"Or if I was blind?
If I get it wrong
Will I lose my mind?"

"Not at all" said Doc
"Eyes open or closed
Trust in the brain
It knows just where to go."

"As you look at the spot
And focus on the feelings
Your brain sees the pain
And then starts the healing."

Brainspotting was beginning to appear more clear
Doc sounded hopeful and Cub felt less fear.

"Doc it makes sense
Well it is starting to
When we look **out**
We're looking **in** too

To release the bad feelings
That have taken control
I look at the stick and just let my mind roll."

"That's it!" smiled Doc
"Your mind can process the mess
So you can feel at your best."

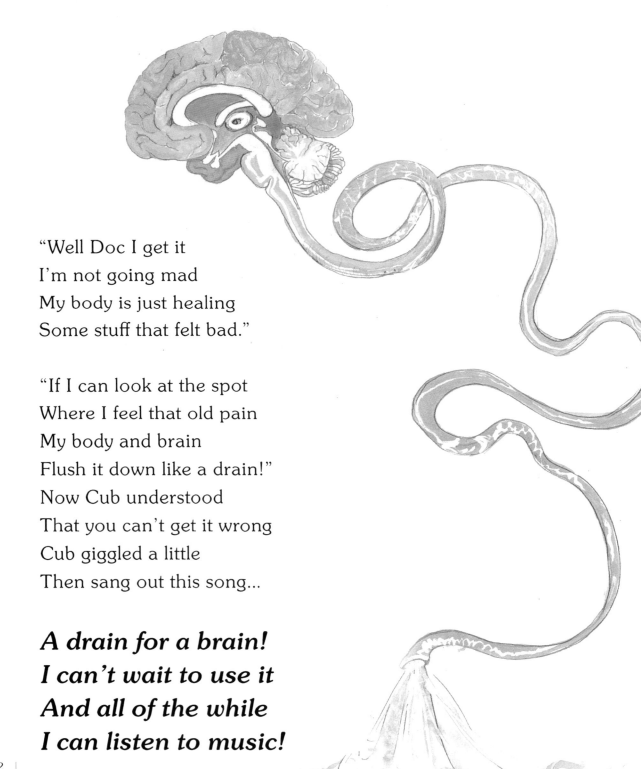

"Well Doc I get it
I'm not going mad
My body is just healing
Some stuff that felt bad."

"If I can look at the spot
Where I feel that old pain
My body and brain
Flush it down like a drain!"
Now Cub understood
That you can't get it wrong
Cub giggled a little
Then sang out this song...

**A drain for a brain!**
**I can't wait to use it**
**And all of the while**
**I can listen to music!**

# TRYING OUT BRAINSPOTTING

Cub went on to say
Why they came here today
"Everything's weird
I just don't feel okay."

"I think I should tell you
But I don't know how
Talking about it feels
Like it's happening now!"

"The memories are back
And it all feels too real
Confusion and sickness
Tummy spinning like a wheel!"

Doc comforted Cub
"Strong feelings are okay
This stuff's in the past now
You're safe here today."

Bear Cub sure was brave
Drew a picture of the worry
On went the headphones
Nice and easy – no hurry.

"Okay" said brave Bear Cub
Focussed on the spot
At the tip of the stick
Wondering what might happen
As it all felt quite new
Thinking of weird memories
And looking at the bamboo.

Cub stayed with the feelings
Felt an awkward pain
But carried on watching like a video game.

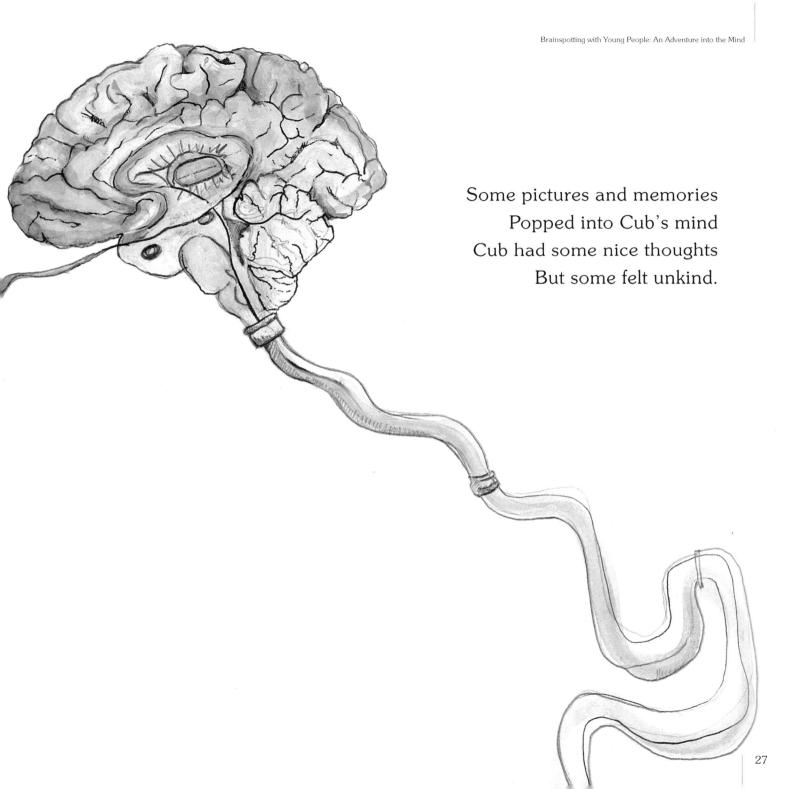

Some pictures and memories
Popped into Cub's mind
Cub had some nice thoughts
But some felt unkind.

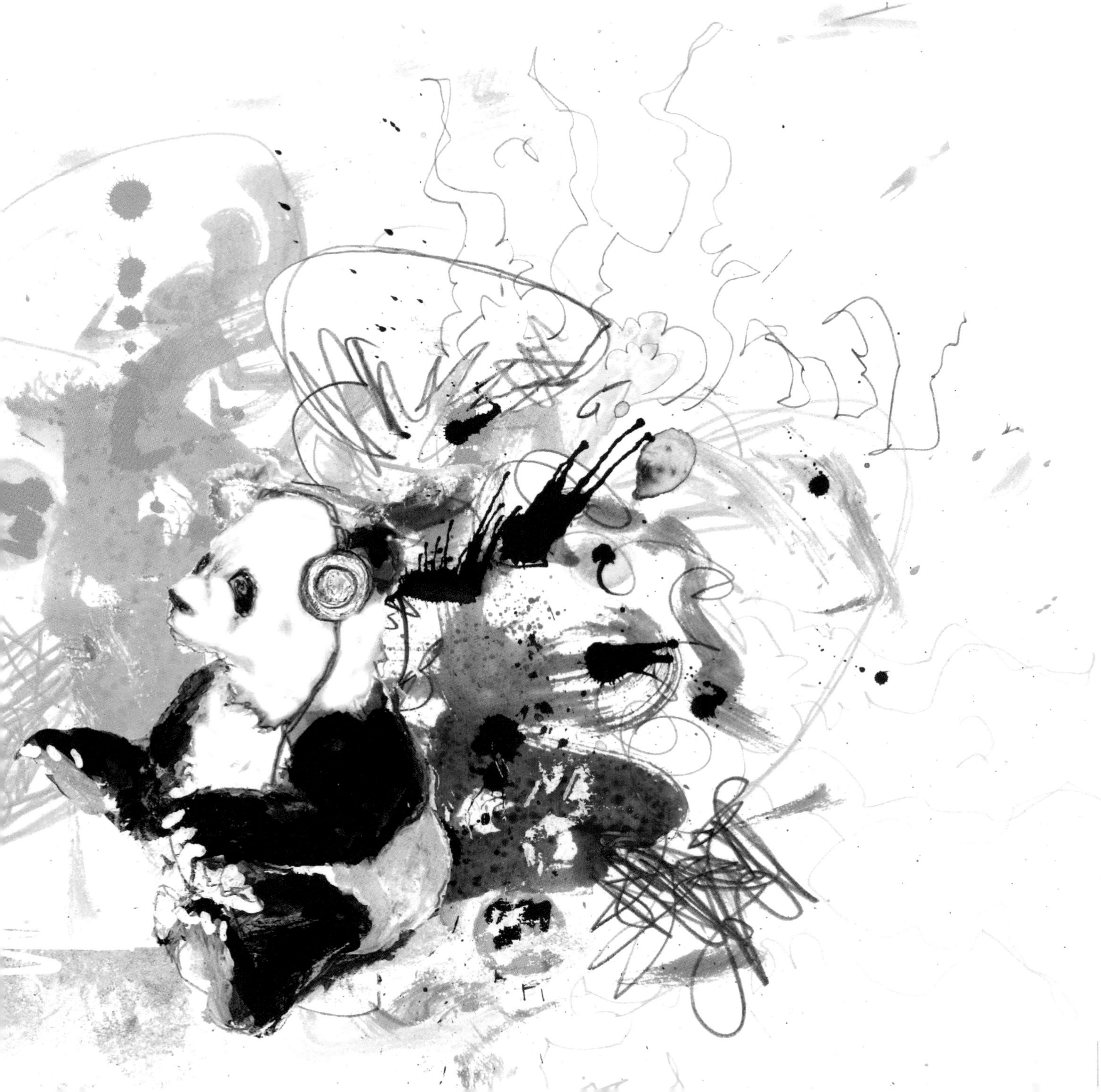

After a while it felt easier
Less tense
Cub noticed the stuff
Was making more sense.

It wasn't like magic
Where things disappear
Just kinder and gentler
Without all the fear.

Cub's face grew softer
As out went the hurt
Took a deep breath
And let out a big...

Cub smiled kind of cheeky
And spoke with surprise
From the tip of the stick
Cub shifted both eyes.

Cub looked straight at Doc
"I feel kind of strange
It's as if some things
Have been rearranged."

"Not in a bad way
Well let me explain
Like having a friendly
Body and brain."

"The worrying thoughts
Feel smaller, okay
I feel more relaxed
Like I just want to play."

Well this was good news
And Bear Cub did play
Excited and happy
For the rest of the day.

## FEELING GOOD

Over the weeks
The bears saw Doc again

Sometimes they walked there
Sometimes took the train.

Each time was different
Doc had lots of ideas
Little by little
The fears disappeared.

Bursting with happiness
"You're as cheeky as ever,"
Laughed happy Big Bear
As they hugged close together.

Big Bear and Bear Cub
Had lots of great times
They laughed every time
Bear Cub sang out the rhyme:

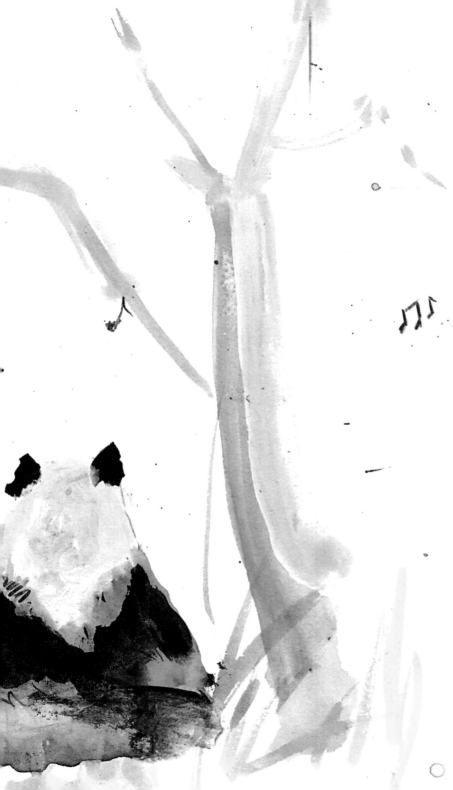

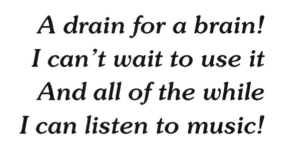

*A drain for a brain!*
*I can't wait to use it*
*And all of the while*
*I can listen to music!*

Before much too long
Poly-vagal learned the song
Singing it strong
As Doc hummed along.

So we saw with Brainspotting
You go with the flow
Where your mind goes
Nobody knows.

That's just like this story
As quite a few times
You will have heard
How it flows using rhymes.

Do all stories rhyme?
Do all feelings flow?
Some people say yes
Some people say...

...probably not.

Made in the USA
Charleston, SC
23 May 2016